DEALING EFFECTIVELY WITH THE MEDIA

John Wade

A FIFTY-MINUTE™ SERIES BOOK

CRISP PUBLICATIONS, INC.
Menlo Park, California

DEALING EFFECTIVELY WITH THE MEDIA

John Wade

CREDITS:
Editor: **Tony Hicks**
Layout and Composition: **ExecuStaff**
Cover Design: **Carol Harris**
Cartoons: **Ralph Mapson**

Distribution to the U.S. Trade:

National Book Network, Inc.
4720 Boston Way
Lanham, MD 20706
1-800-462-6420

Library of Congress Catalog Card Number 91-76239
Wade, John
Dealing Effectively with the Media
ISBN 1-56052-116-3

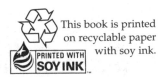
This book is printed on recyclable paper with soy ink.

PREFACE

The Good News

The media are everywhere! And they are ravenous in their appetites for people and ideas. Publications of all sorts and radio and television outlets *must* fill millions of pages and millions of minutes of broadcast time each week. The flow of written and spoken words rushes forth daily, always increasing, never stopping!

No matter who you are or what you do, you will be involved in some of this media activity. Oh, you *may* escape, but it's highly unlikely. The chances are excellent that you will be a participant in some manner, willingly or unwillingly, on a radio or television program, or that you will be the subject of, or a quoted source in, a printed article.

The enormous appetites of the media actually translate into good news and opportunities for you. The precise point of this book is that you can benefit from this situation, both personally and professionally. You just need to be properly trained and thoroughly prepared—and this book shows you how.

You may be abruptly confronted by a reporter, or you may be interviewed in a leisurely manner on a long-scheduled television or radio talk show, or for a newspaper or magazine article. In each of these situations you will be dealing with a professional, a man or woman who is experienced in gathering information of all kinds from a wide range of people in short periods of time. To face media people on a basis of equality, you have every right and obligation to arm yourself with all available weapons. In fact, you must do this in order to be effective!

This book is designed to rid you of any feelings of hesitancy or trepidation you may have. It will provide you with the fundamental knowledge and skills you will need to be comfortable, confident, and effective in all your dealings with any sector of the media at any level.

The satisfaction you can derive from using a media encounter to your company's advantage—or for your own career advancement, or to win over a large audience to ideas or goals you hold dear, or just for personal prestige—is beyond description.

You can have that satisfaction!

John Wade

ABOUT THE AUTHOR

During the past twenty years, John Wade has interviewed thousands of people on local, national, and international television programs. As an award-winning host, he has questioned and conversed with every imaginable type of guest, from presidents and famous actors to animal trainers and eccentric inventors. The topics he has covered range from the most serious and tragic to the most frivolous and funny. He has often been interviewed on radio and television, and he has been the subject of many articles and features in print. He has taught television on-camera performance classes within the industry and for university students. His credits include appearances on ''The Tonight Show,'' being a frequent panelist on the nationally syndicated ''To Tell The Truth'' game show, and five seasons of hosting live satellite videoconferences on business management. He has also appeared in over five hundred television commercials.

CONTENTS

P A R T

I

Introduction

This book is for practically everybody—men and women in all walks of life, in every profession and industry, in large and small organizations, at all levels of responsibility. It is also for those, in or out of the business world, who have convictions, causes, services, or talents about which they feel strongly.

Whether you choose to get into a media situation or it is thrust upon you, the beginning point in preparing to be effective is forming the right attitude.

THE RIGHT ATTITUDE

Every media contact should be thought of as an opportunity. Seldom do any two people have exactly the same pattern in their contacts and opportunities. One person may deal exclusively with newspaper reporters, another only with talk show producers and hosts on radio, a third only with television news personnel. Many people will have frequent contacts with all three sectors of the media; others will have sporadic dealings with one or two sectors. Some of these dealings will be on a national or regional level. Most will be on a local level.

Whatever the contact on whatever level, *from your standpoint,* any dealing with radio, television, or the print medium is important!

> When *you* are involved, there are *no* unimportant interviews, articles, comments, or quotes.

Consider the potential impact of each of the media events listed below. Read all the descriptions, then decide which of the four events is the most important. Write the reason for your conclusion in the space provided.

1. A taped, prime time network television interview with the CEO of the nation's leading automobile manufacturing company.

2. A live, two-hour, radio call-in show featuring opposing candidates for a council seat in a city with a population of 400,000.

3. A full-page article with photos in the local newspaper about a woman who owns and runs the only day-care center in a town of 5,700 people.

4. A 45-second television interview (edited from four minutes) on the evening news with a mother who is concerned about toxic waste being dumped near a park where her children regularly play.

I think the most important of these four media events is _____

because _____ .

See the next page for a discussion of these four events.

HOW RIGHT WAS YOUR ATTITUDE?

Many people conclude that the most important of these events would be the first since the broadcast would be seen nationwide by millions of people. There's a certain plausibility to that conclusion. However, *for you* to come to that conclusion would be incorrect.

There are, of course, many vantage points from which to view media happenings. But if you are to deal effectively with the media, you must view such events *from the standpoints of the persons participating*.

For the persons involved in our examples, *all four media events are of equal importance!* Let's examine them.

In the *first case*, the CEO has a lot on the line. How he comes across could potentially help or hinder sales, make or break his career, and profoundly affect the lives of everyone who works for the company.

In the *second case*, the political future of each candidate could hang on one answer or a careless aside during the program. The lives of the candidates' families could change drastically based upon how each personality strikes the listening voters.

In the *third case*, what could be more important than the reputation of a day-care center in a small town? The very livelihood and future of the woman in the third case ride on the impression she makes on the writer of the article and the resultant story told in words and pictures.

In the *fourth case*, the living conditions for an entire neighborhood may depend on the ability of one mother to put into a few words what all mothers feel about the safety and health of their children.

Is the national television interview more important to the prominent CEO than the newspaper article is to the owner of the day-care center? Certainly not! Is the radio face-off more important to the candidates than the quick few seconds of exposure are to the mother who is concerned about the health of her children? Certainly not!

Each person in the four examples felt that the particular media event in which he or she was involved was of the utmost importance. *This is exactly how you should feel* each and every time you deal with the media, even when your exposure time is limited or the subject seems trivial. With this attitude, you'll always do your best. And participating in one media event could lead to participating in more . . . or none!

> Never underestimate how much media exposure could benefit or harm you.

P A R T

II

Understanding the Media

Your ability to deal effectively with any subject is directly related to how much you know about that subject. The more you understand, the more you are comfortable dealing with any aspect of that subject. The need to understand the media has been demonstrated on a national level many times over. Recall the Kennedy/Nixon and Bush/Dukakis confrontations on television—these are famous examples of what happens when one person understands and uses television while the other doesn't.

A person who anticipates being a part of any media presentation should learn as much as possible about the media in general as well as each specific sector of the media. With so much riding on how well you do, you can't afford to be uninformed.

We're all exposed to the media so frequently that we are quite familiar with their end products—broadcast programs, newspapers, periodicals, trade journals. Many of us therefore assume that we also know a great deal about the workings of the media and their personnel. That assumption isn't always correct.

Take the simple true/false test on the next page to get an idea of where you stand regarding some general media facts.

HOW MUCH DO YOU KNOW ABOUT THE MEDIA?

Read each of the following statements and decide whether it is true or false. Write ''T'' or ''F'' in the space provided.

_____ 1. Taken as a group, people working in the media in the United States are generally representative of the nation's population with regard to race, religion, and lifestyle preferences.

_____ 2. The credentials of guest experts appearing on TV and radio programs are normally verified by production staff members.

_____ 3. It has been demonstrated by research that if broadcast and print journalists are biased in any way, they are able to keep those personal biases from influencing their work.

_____ 4. Among media decision makers the number of conservatives and liberals is about even.

_____ 5. If you have been the subject of a newspaper article or magazine feature, you can expect that the writer of the piece will run it by you before it appears in print.

_____ 6. Truth is the media's first requirement when choosing content for programs and publications.

_____ 7. It has been shown that on controversial issues the media are generally quite fair at showing both sides, giving equal time and space to each.

_____ 8. During television and radio call-in programs, callers are put on-the-air in the order in which they call.

_____ 9. Most general managers of TV and radio stations are more experienced in the area of programming than sales.

_____ 10. Traditionally, the media and business get along very well.

ANSWERS, NEXT PAGE

ANSWERS

All ten statements about the media are false!

If you had nine or ten correct responses, it's an indication that you're generally well-informed about the media. Most people are not. There are many startling facts about the media which the average person doesn't know.

The remainder of this chapter is devoted to increasing your knowledge about the media. Your awareness of these important facts will bear directly on your effectiveness before, during, and after your actual participation in a media event.

THE POWER OF THE MEDIA

Just a couple of decades ago the term ''the media'' wasn't familiar to most adults. Now even children know the term and realize the power it suggests.

From what source is this power of the media derived? What do you think? (Write your answer here:)

_____

_____

_____

_____

_____

_____

_____

_____

_____

_____

Power suggests the capacity to do work and to act. The media certainly have the capacity to do an enormous amount of work and to act quickly and decisively. However, the power of the media is not derived from a capacity to work or to act. Further, the media's power has nothing to do with how quickly or even how reasonably, accurately, or morally they act.

The media derive their power from another capacity: *the capacity to influence,* to produce effects on others. No one is immune from the influence of the media with their dominating omnipresence. Television, radio, and print are the great informers and teachers of our day. Not only do the media control what words and pictures reach the masses, the media even control, for the most part, their own praise and criticism.

As a person contemplating participating in media events, you should keep this idea of influence uppermost in your mind. You are using a media event to influence readers, viewers, or listeners. From your standpoint, how the media operate or how well is not your concern. (Your concern as a private citizen is another matter.) As a participant, you should be concerned only with making the best use of a media end product.

MEDIA OVERVIEW

With few exceptions, the media are businesses set up to make money for their owners or stockholders. Television and radio stations unceasingly seek higher ratings that translate into more revenue and additional profits. Publishers of printed materials try to improve circulation to increase sales revenue, advertising rates, and profits. Certainly, in the area of trying to maximize profits, the media are much like other businesses.

However, a certain perception of "uniqueness" has developed about the media. This is due to the visibility, prominence, and power of the outlets themselves; the sensitive and important nature of many topics covered; the fame of some owners and personalities working in the various mediums; and the overly competitive nature of the industry. Unfortunately, this perception of uniqueness exists both among the public and within the industry. It tends to make dealing with members of the media a bit more daunting than it really should be, especially in interview situations.

Following is some general information to help you better understand the workings of the media, their goals and priorities, and the characteristics of media personnel. The more you know, the easier it will be for you to recognize if dealing with certain persons on certain subjects might work to your advantage or disadvantage, considering their agendas and values versus yours.

- The goal of television and radio programming is ratings. The goal of newspapers and magazines (including trade journals) is to increase sales. *The content of programs and publications is very often chosen with these goals in mind.* (Naturally, some stories must be covered, regardless of the effect on sales or ratings.)

- Frequently, interviewers (reporters, talk show hosts, journalists) are looking for controversy—something sensational or negative about you, your cause, your company, or your industry. Certainly, you will sometimes deal with programs, publications, and interviewers oriented toward harmony and the positive aspects of your cause or company. Unfortunately, you will run across these less often than you would like.

- Keep in mind that people in the media are seldom writing articles, producing programs, or hosting them merely to collect unchallenged information or opinions that you'd like to dispense. The media are looking first to fill their own needs.

- The media people with whom you will deal are human beings and have their biases. Some can put them aside for the sake of fairness better than others. Unfortunately, the concept of just what fairness is varies greatly from person to person. Certain media biases have been thoroughly documented.

- It is not the purpose of this book to take sides on specific issues; but there is a completely evident obligation to make you aware that definite media biases do exist, so that you can use them to your advantage or thoroughly prepare to combat them and still achieve your goals in media encounters. Information about these biases is readily available. For example, surveys have shown that the vast majority of media employees, especially those in ownership, programming, production, and on-air work, are highly liberal in their views. Few of them hold traditional values or conservative positions on the popular societal, moral, and political issues of our day.

- Minorities are not well-represented in decision-making positions in the media. Further, certain ethnic groups have inordinate media power and representation while others have virtually no participation. The fact that these conditions exist may not directly affect your participation, but being sensitive to this issue could help you on occasion. More importantly, not being aware has the potential to hinder you.

- You'd expect that some on-air radio and television personalities, as well as some successful print journalists, would be self-centered. What you must be prepared to face is that program producers and other staff members occasionally display signs of egos that dwarf those of the on-air performers. Even if you're dealing with people in a small town, there is no assurance that egos will be easier to deal with than on a network show or national publication. It is good to keep this in mind during initial contacts and when deciding on content and the extent of your participation, the length of time allowed, and any other logistical items.

- Always facing deadlines, reporters, writers, and hosts cover many stories and conduct frequent interviews, and much of the content is tragic and depressing. As a result, some frontline media people may seem to lack sensitivity. You may not be treated with the promptness or courtesy you'd like. This usually must be tolerated; it is seldom directed at you personally. Media people are in high-tension, high-pressure jobs. You'll get along better with them if you show them that you are sensitive to this and respect their responsibilities.

MEDIA OVERVIEW (Continued)

- Decision-making power on news broadcasts resides primarily with the news director. On other broadcasts, the producer normally has the final say. On-air people generally have much less say over guests and content than you would think. There are exceptions, more so on radio than television. And of course real ''stars,'' local or national, wield considerable power and influence.

- The person controlling the program on-the-air or writing the article about you may or may not care about you as a human being. That person may or may not be truthful, insightful, intelligent, reliable, or objective. He or she is merely a person, perhaps highly motivated, perhaps not, who is trying to do a job within the limits of talent and attitude. Some in those positions are very competent; some are not.

- Most of the so-called creative people in the media feel that the work they do is, of its nature, *very important.*

THE MEDIA AND BUSINESS

Most readers of this book are likely to be business people who will be participating in media events as part of their work responsibilities. So here are some facts about the relationship between the media and the world of business.

The agendas of the media and business are not naturally compatible, even though the media are themselves businesses with the same ultimate motivation of making money. There has always been distrust between the two entities, even before the advent of television. There is now a wary coexistence with each willing to use the other for possible benefit.

Frequently, cooperation does pay off handsomely for both. The media draw readers, viewers, and listeners with features about businesses that actually result in good public relations and increased profits for those businesses. But the media also draw those same readers, viewers, and listeners with other features about businesses that result in terrible public relations, greatly decreased revenues, and sometimes irreparable harm for those businesses. The media win either way as long as the revealed facts grip the public.

Even though encounters between the media and business are often adversarial, they need not be hostile or negative in tone. When a professional media person armed with business information faces off with a professional business person armed with media information, both can win.

If you aspire to prominence and success in your company, you must be prepared to welcome, or at least tolerate and utilize to advantage, your inevitable exposure to the media. Business leaders who want to continue to lead must deal with the challenge of becoming effective communicators through whatever medium presents itself. Given three people with otherwise equal qualifications, the person with the best communication skills will get the job or the promotion or the public recognition—and the commensurate salary.

Communication skills have always been important in the business world, but those skills used to be exercised mainly within the organization. Outside the company, challenges were usually not much more demanding than typical speaking engagements. Those days are gone forever; the media as they now exist have redefined the requirements necessary to be a total communicator.

> If you cannot deal effectively with the media,
> you are not prepared for the business world of the 1990s.

THE MEDIA AND BUSINESS (Continued)

Besides being the great informers and teachers of our day, the media are also the great intimidators. If the idea of facing a confrontational interviewer on live television about a recent problem within your company scares you half to death, you're normal and part of a large group. Most business people who are otherwise capable share your feeling.

P A R T

III

The Meaning of "Dealing"

Obviously, your personality, appearance, conduct, and delivery of content form the essence of the media impact you will make. However, effectively dealing with the media goes far beyond your ability to do well during a media event.

Although practically all the actual dealings with the media will be yours to control, *the importance of the conduct of anyone acting on your behalf cannot be overemphasized.* Impressions of you, your organization, your ideas, and your attitude are conveyed every time a contact is made with any media employee—whether it's a phone call, a letter, or an in-person visit.

Make certain that everything and everyone associated with you exudes class, courtesy, confidence, and consistency. The reception-ist's comments are sometimes more important to the staff of a program or publication than the comments of the general manager. A negative impression prior to your participation could hinder you.

Even after your participation, a less than cordial exchange between your people and theirs could result in never being asked back and no recommendations to other media outlets. In a small market, your media appearances could well come to an end.

Dealing with the media includes: *every* contact you make with *every* person employed by *any* broadcast or print medium and *every* contact made by *anyone* who represents you or works with you or for you before, during, *and* after any actual participation by you.

HOW MUCH CONTROL?

When dealing with the media, you are an outsider. You must reconcile yourself to not having total control over many aspects of your participation.

For each of the following aspects, indicate how much control you expect to have. Check ''no control,'' ''some,'' ''a lot'' or ''complete control,'' as appropriate.

	No control	Some control	A lot of control	Complete control
Your appearance and attitude	_____	_____	_____	_____
Your words	_____	_____	_____	_____
When and where you'll participate	_____	_____	_____	_____
With whom you'll participate	_____	_____	_____	_____
How long you'll be participating	_____	_____	_____	_____

Look at the next page to see how realistic your expectations are.

REALISTIC OR NOT?

A REALISTIC ASSESSMENT

Control over your appearance and attitude always remains with you.

You also have a lot of control over your words—but remember that a newspaper reporter may not quote you accurately, and a radio or television reporter may decide to edit out much of what you said.

Sometimes you have some say as to when, where and with whom you'll participate, but most times you'll simply be told where you'll participate and when to show up.

Normally you'll have no control over how long you'll be on-the-air. Sometimes you won't even know how long you'll be on unless you ask; and even then, you may not find out, or the time may be changed at the last second—or while you're on-the-air.

Even when dealing with the print medium, when, where and how long are usually not your decisions. You have the least control—only those bare essentials of appearance, attitude, and the words you speak—when a reporter unexpectedly confronts you for a comment on something.

Here are two tips about control:

- Don't waste energy on what you can't control.

- *Before* the event, try to control as many important factors as possible that may benefit you.

YOUR ROLE

It should not surprise you that, since the media control the content and length, and the times and frequencies of publications and broadcasts, they would also want to control you as much as possible. That's why you're not just given a half-hour of prime time or half the front page of the newspaper to do whatever suits you or your organization. This concept of control brings us to the important subject of how you are most likely to be utilized as a media participant.

> Practically every participation for you will be some form of interview.

Your role may be to give one short comment for the evening news about your company's hiring practices. Or you may be the sole guest on a one-hour radio call-in program. Or you may be chosen for a personality profile in the supplement of your Sunday newspaper. In every case, some media person will be present to ask questions, screen phones, limit time, write the final copy, and generally control the flow of interactions to reach the intended goal of the final product.

In rare cases, you may be given a minute of air time to tape a message looking directly into the camera—perhaps to rebut an editorial by the station management. Even in that case, your written copy will be reviewed and must be approved by a producer.

The fact that some type of interviewer will always be present to ask questions and exert control should not upset you. On the contrary, the presence of such a professional actually takes many pressures off you. The interviewer normally has a number of responsibilities besides having to ask the right questions to keep the interview on track. You can direct all your attention to your sole responsibility as the interviewee.

From your standpoint as the interviewee, an interview of any length with a capable interviewer should be a comfortable and invigorating experience. You'll be talking about one of your favorite topics, about which you are knowledgeable (the topic may even be you!). You will have many opportunities to make the positive points for which you've prepared.

YOUR ROLE (Continued)

There will be times when the interviewer, for any number of reasons, will be a hindrance to you in reaching your interview goals. Many times, however, the interviewer, whatever his or her view of the subject, will be of considerable help. The interviewer will keep you focused and will insist upon succinct and substantive answers to his or her questions.

- Welcome the interview challenge.

- Master your role as the interviewee.

- Be just as good in your role as the interviewer is in his or her role.

P A R T

IV

Media Interviews

It is very important to understand just what print, radio, and television interviews can and cannot do.

Most times, of course, you are not able to choose the type of interview in which you will participate. You are normally asked, or confronted, by a station or publication representative. When you become more experienced, you may sometimes initiate contact yourself, thereby selecting the medium and format best suited to your strengths and your message (see Part 8). The ultimate goal is to be equally effective in all sectors of the media.

ARE ALL INTERVIEWS EQUAL?

In the sentences that follow, fill in each blank with one of these words:

radio
TV
news (in any medium)
print

1. Generally, I'll be given the most time to express myself in a _____ interview.

2. I'm most likely to be caught off-guard in my remarks in a _____ interview.

3. The most risk of being perceived inaccurately by the public results from doing a _____ interview.

4. I have an opportunity to make the greatest impact on the public by doing a _____ interview.

5. If I'm knowledgeable about my company's services but have a poor memory for details, dates, and figures, I'd probably be at my best in a _____ interview.

6. My personality is most likely to be accurately revealed in a _____ interview.

7. The most challenging and difficult type of interview is the _____ interview.

8. Generally, I'll be most pressed for time while doing a _____ interview.

9. My rapport with the interviewer is most important in a _____ interview.

10. Of the three media, more of my message is likely to get across accurately using a _____ interview.

ANSWERS →

25

Dealing Effectively with the Media

ANSWERS— MEDIA INTERVIEW QUIZ

The correct answers are:

1. *Print.* You will normally spend a good deal more time actually talking with the writer of an article than you would with a broadcast host or newsperson. Depending upon the length of the article and the nature of the publication, you could spend hours or even days with the interviewer. Interviews could take place in your office or theirs, your home, a restaurant, or any number of places. Some interviews or parts of interviews are done by phone. You'll normally have plenty of time to express yourself—but you can never be sure of how much of what you have said will be printed.

2. *Print.* The length of time spent with a print person tends to put you in a more relaxed mood than you would be in with a broadcast person. TV or radio broadcasts and tapings, with their time limitations and audiences of viewers or listeners, keep you alert to always saying the right thing. Print interviews have built-in dangers.

   Frequently during print interviews a meal break is taken where considerable socializing takes place. Inexperienced people may assume that what is said during this time is not part of the interview process. Also, many off-guard remarks are made just as the interview meeting breaks up and you are saying good-bye. Once again, an inexperienced person may assume that the formal proceedings have ended. They haven't!

   A good media person never stops gathering potentially useful information. Even if the person says, ''Thank you, it's over''—don't let down your guard!

3. *Print.* Readers don't actually see or hear you. The writer's impressions of you are what the reader absorbs. Quotes may be passed on to the readers only in part, out of context, or even inaccurately. *Print interviews are more risky than you might at first think.* The content and slant of the final article are highly unpredictable.

4. *TV.* The viewers actually see you and hear your words. If the interview is live, the viewers will hear your unedited words.

5. *Radio.* Normally, you may take along as many notes and papers as you'd like. Your answers are what the listeners hear. They may or may not be aware that you are using references. Usually, the listeners don't care and neither does the radio host. He or she just wants a good show.

   During a print interview, on the other hand, if you frequently use references the writer may perceive you as uncertain or unknowledgeable.

6. **TV.** Neither radio nor print can approach television, especially live television, in revealing aspects of your personality as they truly are. Some people may be more relaxed during a radio interview, and thus feel that they are revealing more of their personality, but television can show the whole personality in a way that radio cannot rival.

7. **TV.** Particularly if the interview is broadcast live, you must have it all together—your words, appearance, and attitude.

8. **News.** You can generally count on news interviews being much shorter than other interviews. The main reasons are the immediacy of news; the resultant urgency of deadlines; and the short attention span of viewers, listeners, or readers.

9. **Print.** On radio and TV you make your own impression on the public by your performance. Certainly it helps to have a good rapport with the broadcast interviewer. However, the ultimate impact you make will be your responsibility, and you can make a positive impression on listeners or viewers no matter what the rapport between you and the interviewer.

   In a print interview, your success is very dependent upon what the interviewer thinks of you. Rapport with a print interviewer is crucial. If the rapport is good, you are more likely to be written about in a positive manner.

   (*Note:* During taped broadcast interviews that are going to be edited, establishing a good rapport with the interviewer could result in a final tape more advantageous to you.)

10. **Radio.** Television gets across more of your personality than your message. Viewers tend to form a general impression of you rather than to retain details. Print is *capable* of getting your message across in great detail; but unless you write the article yourself, what gets to the readers may not be as accurate or as complete as you would like.

    Radio is the most likely of the three to correctly get a message across in detail. Naturally, if the radio interview is not live and has been edited, some of your message will be lost.

CHARACTERISTICS OF MEDIA INTERVIEWS

The general characteristics of media interviews are listed below.

A television interview

—gets across more of your personality, but less of your message.

—is actually you saying what you choose to say.

—if taped, may result in part of what you say being edited out.

—usually allows less time for you to speak than print or radio, sometimes only a matter of seconds.

A radio interview

—gets across more of your message, but less of your personality.

—is actually you saying what you choose to say.

—if taped, may result in part of what you say being edited out.

—usually allows less time for you to speak than print but more than television, sometimes only a matter of seconds.

A print interview

—*may* get your message across in some detail, and *may* accurately reveal aspects of your personality as well.

—usually allows more time for you to speak than television or radio.

—results in someone writing their impressions of you and of what you *may* have said.

—sometimes fails to capture the attitude and nuances of your delivery. Things you say (particularly if they are humorous or said "tongue-in-cheek") may not read the same in print. Readers can't see your smile.

TYPES OF INTERVIEWS

A media interview can be one question and a brief answer—or a conversation over many hours that covers a wide variety of topics.

A broadcast news interview normally reaches a larger audience than an interview on any other type of program, but exposure time is usually very brief. Exposure time on a talk show, for example, would be considerably longer than on a news program, but fewer people would normally be watching.

A situation may arise where you would be required to give a number of interviews on basically the same issue. Such interviews could be back-to-back during a period of a few hours, or extended over a period of months. To add variety or to ease the boredom of being repetitive, there is the temptation to change your answers or restate your message. You *must* resist the tendency to do this. Take each interview as the first—it is for the interviewer—and keep your same phraseology and attitude.

Most television, radio, and print interviews can be divided into two broad categories. An interview either is basically a *personality profile* or is concerned primarily with *subject matter*. Of course, some interviews will mix the two to some extent. You should be well aware of the type you will be involved in long before the interview begins. Indicators are the style of the interviewer or writer, and the program format or nature of the publication. If you're in doubt, ask in plenty of time so that you can properly prepare.

Print Interviews

Some characteristics of print interviews:

- Normally conducted in person, one-on-one, sometimes with more than one meeting.

- On occasion, more frequently than in the past, may be conducted by telephone either entirely or in combination with in-person contacts.

- There may be an exchange of written or printed material involving opinions and/or facts and statistics.

- Locations vary greatly (if you get to select, pick a place where you are comfortable!).

TYPES OF INTERVIEWS (Continued)

Radio and TV Interviews

On radio and television, whether you are interviewed as the sole guest or with other guests, you will usually be interviewed by one person. Two or more interviewers may, however, be present in a press conference, a scheduled topical news special, or a co-hosted talk show.

Television and radio interviews can be:

- *Live*

- *Live-on-tape:* The program is taped, but played back in its entirety at a later broadcast time.

- *Taped and edited:* Very little or almost all of what was said could be deleted.

- *Taped, edited, and broadcast out of sequence:* What material remains after editing is broadcast in the order selected by the program producer.

The radio and TV interviews that you will most commonly encounter are the following or some combination of the following:

- In studio with interviewer(s)

- On location with interviewer(s)—any area, indoors or outdoors, other than the studio

- Remote straight-to-camera or straight-to-microphone—you are not physically present with interviewer(s)

- Face-to-face, one-on-one with interviewer

- Panel—face-to-face, with interviewer(s), with at least one other guest present

- Pro-con—face-to-face with one person having an opposing view, with a moderator present

- By telephone

- With audience questions—audience either physically present or by telephone

- Abrupt encounter with interviewer(s)—as you leave work or the courthouse, at a disaster site, etc.

- Program where you are paid as a guest, speaker, or expert presenter—usually for a profit-oriented industrial video program; you are not normally paid when appearing as "yourself" on commercial radio or television .

> TV is mightier than the pen (or radio).

The most challenging of all media interviews is a *live television interview.* If done well, it is by far the most effective of all interviews a business person, or person with a cause, can give. Every element for impact is present:

- You can be seen

- and heard

- saying what you choose to say

- in context

- without the risk of anything being deleted.

P A R T

V

Before the Interview

How well you do in any interview will depend a great deal on what you do *before* the interview. Whether you are going to be interviewed on television, radio, or for a print publication, the key to doing well is—preparation. You should never attempt to handle a scheduled media interview without thoroughly preparing for it. To wing it is, at best, to lose an opportunity to advance yourself, your company or cause. At worst, your lack of preparation could result in a catastrophic public relations problem and irreparable harm to your organization and your career.

On occasion, you may be confronted abruptly by a reporter who gives you no warning. But this happening should in no way surprise you! Given the fact that a reporter wants to talk with you or some other representative of your organization or cause means someone believes there is a *story*. You should always have at least one or two statements that would both satisfy a reporter and place your organization in a positive light. Stay constantly prepared for abrupt confrontational interviews if your job, or area of business, or personal activity is of a sensitive nature to the media and the public.

The fact that you are to be interviewed could have come about for any number of reasons. You may be the obvious spokesperson for a particular subject or problem. You may have made the media contact yourself in an attempt to publicize a specific product, service or change of policy. Another person familiar with your area of expertise may have mentioned your name to a media source.

It makes no difference how you came to be the interviewee. *You must be dedicated to a thorough preparation process.* As you become more experienced in being interviewed, you'll come to know just what "thorough preparation" means for you.

PART V
BEFORE THE INTERVIEW (Continued)

The remainder of this chapter will outline a preparation process that will cover all the bases. If you diligently follow this process before each media interview, you'll have every reason to feel relaxed, comfortable, and confident when the interview begins—because you'll be thoroughly prepared.

WHO SHOULD SPEAK?

The first step in preparing for a media interview is a major one. Should you or should you not actually do the interview? Unfortunately, many times not enough deliberation is given to this question. Perhaps you are not the right person for the interview that is scheduled.

Every organization should have a set of detailed guidelines for selecting the correct spokespersons in specific and sensitive areas. The organization should also provide thorough training at every level for the people who are selected. Since most companies still do not recognize the importance of solid media relations, the responsibilities of being a media spokesperson usually fall to someone in the public relations department. Many PR people are very good in this role, highly motivated, well-trained, and experienced. But they are not the most sought after by the media as interviewees.

In the absence of guidelines set by your organization, use the following sound general considerations when making that first major decision of who should represent a company, or a cause, in each particular media interview.

SOUND COMPANY RULES

- Provide the top person available. The media and the public are impressed with the highest ranking executives.

- Make certain that the person is knowledgeable enough to handle all possible questions.

- Select a person who has the authority and discretion to discuss sensitive information beyond the specific subject or problem at hand.

- Send someone who personifies the image of the company you want before the public.

- If possible, only allow a person to speak for your company who has been trained to handle the media interview challenge.

- Use a PR person only as a last resort and only if she or he meets all the previous criteria.

Sometimes it's impossible to meet all of these requirements, but an organization should always strive to do so.

> How you come across in the media becomes the public perception of you and your company or cause.

FIRST CONTACT

When a contact is first made with you or your office about the possibility of your participating in a scheduled media interview, be mindful of the following considerations:

1. Don't be pushed or pressured into making a decision at that very moment—unless, of course, you are familiar with the program or publication contacting you and already know that you would like to participate. Buy yourself a bit of time to think about the offer. Any of the accepted business practices or ploys you use to put off replying immediately will normally work with the media.

2. Before replying, give yourself ample time to decide if you are the right person for the interview, if the program or publication is a good match for your company or your message, and if your appearance at this time would be most advantageous.

3. Usually the person calling you doesn't expect an immediate answer unless that person is working on an urgent news story for that day's broadcast. A reporter may try to use a deadline pressure to try to influence you, but you are not obligated to solve the reporter's problem if doing so might damage you, your message, or your company.

4. Take the time to check out anyone who purports to be a reporter or journalist. *Never do an interview over the telephone until you have verified the person's credentials.* You can do this by calling the place where the person is employed.

5. Avoid at all costs dismissing the media caller without the courtesy of an explanation. If you are able, help the person find another possible interviewee, perhaps a person with a similar viewpoint for your cause or someone from your company better suited to handle the particular interview subject.

6. If you decide not to do the interview, give the media person a good reason why. If your organization can't provide somcone suitable, explain why.

7. If you are not going to do this particular interview, lay the groundwork for a continuing relationship now that you have a media contact. Ask the person to call you again when another need arises.

8. If the media person contacting you is seeking a comment from you to use as a quote on a topical issue, or if he or she wants a quick interview on a current sensitive matter, *never respond "No comment."* To be associated in any area of the news with the words "No comment," or "A company spokesperson refused to comment," is to be perceived by the public and the media as having something to hide that is very negative, not in the public interest, or downright dishonest. Publicity of this kind is exactly what any individual or company doesn't need.

MAKING YOUR DECISION

At some juncture, you will have to decide whether or not it's in your best interest to participate as you have been invited to do. The more information you can obtain about the interview, the better judgment you'll make.

On the following page is a list of questions to ask of your media contact. You should politely and firmly ask as many of the questions as you can. You'll probably not get all your questions answered, but it's best to try and get as much information as possible.

Usually, only the barest essentials are available before you have to decide whether to accept or turn down the interview. The producer of the program or the writer of the article is putting all the pieces together and may not be able to give you any information beyond the subject matter and a tentative date. You may withhold your decision pending more complete details, but you risk being replaced if you are too demanding. It all boils down to your importance to them and the relative importance to you of participating in the media event.

As the interview date grows closer, most of your questions will be answered; but the sooner you know the answers the more it helps you in preparing. If you've developed a good rapport with your media contact, the information you need will be given to you as soon as it's available.

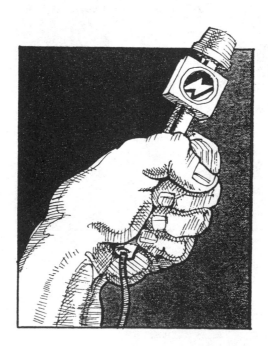

QUESTIONS TO ASK

What date is the interview scheduled?

Where?

What time?

If print: How long will the interview take?

If broadcast: How many minutes will I have?

What is the proposed content?

Why this content?

Why me?

What was the source of your information about me?

Who will be the interviewer(s)?

Any other people involved as guests or subjects? Who?

What is the format of the program or article?

Any idea of the line of questioning at this time?

If radio or television: Will the interview be live, taped, edited? Audience present? Questions from them? Call-ins?

If television: Can props be used (charts, pictures, products, etc.)?

If television: Is the use of film clips or videotape inserts planned? If so, when will I get the opportunity to view them in enough time to prepare comments or responses?

What should I bring with me?

May I bring friends or associates along with me?

START YOUR PREPARATION

When enough information is available, and you have accepted the invitation to participate, start your preparation. Don't wait for every detail about the media event before you begin to outline your goals and approach. All you really need to know is:

- What radio or television program or what publication

- Whether it's a personality or subject-matter interview

- If subject-matter, what that subject matter is

- The general direction of questioning

- An idea of how much time will be allotted for the interview

As you obtain more details about the event, you can work that information into your preparation planning. If necessary, you can adapt your approach to include other guests, a shorter time frame, or whatever changes present themselves.

Part of your preparation time should be spent in learning as much as you can about the person(s) who will be interviewing you. Watch that particular news reporter or anchorperson. Watch the television talk show you're going to be on, or listen to the radio program, and zero in on the host's style. Read a number of articles by the writer to whom you'll be giving information vital to your career or to the success of your company. Watch, listen, and read—and you'll know more about the interviewer's abilities, attitudes, and approach to business than he or she will know about you when the interview begins.

YOUR GOALS VERSUS THEIR GOALS

As you begin your preparation, remember that the media are looking first to fill their own needs. Their biggest need is to provide stimulating television, controversial radio, and exciting articles and features.

While you're calmly trying to tell about the positive aspects of yourself and your company, product, service, or cause, the media are trying to create "great media." They have their goals and you have yours. They are actually more storytellers and provocateurs than they are fact gatherers. If you realize this, you can help them create their great media and still get across your facts and feelings.

Many people participate in media events and are unable or unwilling to adapt their styles to fit the media and their needs. As a result, they are ineffective in getting their messages across. If you understand the dynamics involved and have prepared with specific goals in mind, there is nothing to prevent an interview from being basically satisfying to all parties involved.

Knowing that the interview you want to give may not be the interview the media person is hoping to get should not deter you in the least. In fact, it is one of your responsibilities to yourself and the interview process to understand the interviewer's job as fully as you can and to cooperate in helping him or her do it well up to the point where helping too much would keep you from reaching your goals.

THE PRIORITIZED LIST CONCEPT

To achieve any goal, it is imperative to have that goal clearly in mind. When preparing for an important media interview (there are no unimportant media interviews), this maxim must be taken to its ultimate development.

> Your goals for each interview must be clearly delineated.
> You must be able to describe them with precision—in writing!

Some consultants who train politicians and business people for television interviews advise having in mind three main points to make in an interview. Other consultants say to plan an overall message, then distill it. These approaches are a bit too general in nature, especially to cover interviews of varying lengths or interviews that are shortened just before they are to begin.

The Prioritized List Concept (PLC) has been designed to be used as the *primary tool in preparing for television interviews. The PLC should also be used in preparing for radio and print interviews.* Since notes and other sources may be used during radio and print interviews, merely omit the step requiring memorization.

THE PLC FOR TELEVISION

Develop a prioritized list by following these four steps:

1. Draw up a complete list of the points you want to get across during the interview.

2. Put the most important point first, and so on down the line.

3. After drawing up your prioritized list, edit or outline it to the very briefest form.

4. Commit the brief list to memory.

The reasons for these four systematic moves are to plant the priorities firmly in your mind, to make it necessary to memorize only a few simple items, and to enable you to adapt easily to a last-second reduction of the allotted time for your interview, should that occur.

To illustrate: You've been told an interview will be twelve minutes in duration. You've settled on seven major points you want to drive home. You've clearly and fully written out all seven points, then listed them in order of importance. In your editing, you've distilled the list to one key word or a very few key words per point. You commit the brief list to memory.

Just before you go on-the-air, you're told that your interview will be only five minutes in length. What do you do? Mentally cut your brief form from the bottom up, lopping off the last three points. You have your top four firmly in mind and can concentrate on getting them across.

With practice, you'll be able to gauge how many points you're likely to cover in a certain number of minutes. As a guide only, to help you learn the PLC, you might list only two or three points for a short news interview, and perhaps six or seven points for an interview on a talk show or public service program allotted ten to fifteen minutes.

On the next two pages is an example of how a prioritized list should be developed.

EXAMPLES AHEAD

44

Example of a PLC

Program: "Mid-day Live," Channel 12, noon 8/24
Host: Doris Holmgren. Producer: Rick Finn, 871-1212
Approx. 12 minutes
Points to get across during the interview
1. Convince viewers that Interkonko is an environmentally conscious and socially responsible local company.
   Examples:
   - Most up-to-date factory exhaust devices in the industry that eliminate air pollutants
   - Buildings and landscaping designed and built by local architects and workmen to fit in with surroundings (rolling hills just west of town)
   - Scholarship programs for disadvantaged youth of community
2. Make viewers aware of our new product line just out. (Ask Rick re using our photographs.)
3. Increased employment opportunities due to planned expansion — 230 in various positions.
4. Working conditions at company:
   - Non-union, but higher pay than union
   - Career opportunities, promotion from within
   - Day-care center
   - Maternity and paternity leaves
   - Excellent medical and pension benefits
   - Clean and safe work areas
5. Incoming CEO, Douglas Garner, came up through the ranks with parent company, 34 years.

6. New government regulations that will increase production costs.

7. Actual description of expansion plans (obtain information and stats). Sketch to studio?

Commit to memory:

1. Environmentally / socially responsible / local
   - Exhausts
   - Buildings and landscaping
   - Scholarships
2. New products
3. Employment opportunities — 210
4. Conditions
   - Pay
   - Promotion
   - Day-care
   - Leaves
   - Benefits
   - Work areas
5. CEO
6. Gov't regulations
7. Expansion

46

DISCUSSION OF THE PLC EXAMPLE
(pages 44–45)

In the preceding example of a PLC, it is clear that the main goal of the company representative is to establish a solid image for his organization. He feels that this goal is even more important than the free advertising he will get showing and describing his company's new line of products. Having firmly established his first priority, he will be able to adjust comfortably if the host never gets to the products or brushes over them lightly, or if the producer decides at the last minute not to use the photos.

The content to be committed to memory is quite short and easily remembered. If the company spokesperson has done his homework well, key words are all that need be remembered. They will spark what additional information is needed.

If he remembers that his third point is ''Employment opportunities—210,'' he will be able to tie that in with a mention of the proposed expansion and the fact that various jobs will be available. Then some of those positions will come to mind by name as he speaks. In the same manner, if he remembers ''Leaves'' as an example of his fourth point, he couldn't help but remember to stress that his company is one of the rare ones thinking of fathers.

The PLC, or any other system for that matter, will not be of any help unless the person is *thoroughly prepared*. The purpose of the final memorized PLC outline is to help you easily keep your priorities straight and to *prompt* additional information that will fill in the details. There will only be something to prompt if you have read, reviewed, and assimilated the details. You must know your material.

A person of average intelligence who is generally well-informed on a subject or issue need not memorize every little detail to do well in a television interview. In fact, if everything is committed to memory, the average person cannot relax. If you're not relaxed, it's difficult to go with the natural give-and-take of conversation that is so effective in making an impact on viewers. The premise of the PLC is: ''Know a lot, memorize very little, then relax.''

No interview progresses in a sequence that anyone could possibly envision. In most exchanges there will be a natural place for each of your points, but certainly not in your PLC order. Depending upon the questions of the interviewer, you might not get to your main goal until well into the time allotted. But by being aware of your priorities and having keywords to trigger the content, you can select to bring up the most important point of those you haven't already covered.

YOUR PLC

Assume you are given twelve minutes on live television with your best local news anchorperson. On the following two pages, prioritize a list of points you would like to make about your company, your cause or yourself. Then, as in the example provided earlier, edit or outline your list into the briefest form possible that still contains enough key words to elicit all the necessary information for the interview. Commit your brief prioritized list to memory.

Remember, the points you are to put down are *your* goals to achieve in the interview. List the points you want to make, regardless of the line of questioning.

Your PLC:

Points to Get Across during the Interview: (Must be complete and prioritized)

YOUR PLC (Continued)

Commit to memory: (Briefest form possible)

_____

_____

_____

_____

_____

_____

_____

_____

_____

_____

_____

_____

_____

_____

_____

_____

_____

_____

_____

_____

_____

CHECKLIST

Now answer the following questions about your PLC. Check "yes" or "no" as appropriate.

- Can you easily remember the final outline?   Yes _____ No _____

- Can you easily move from point to point in any order?   Yes _____ No _____

- Would you be able to keep track that you and the interviewer had touched on points 3 and 5, but had not covered the others?   Yes _____ No _____

- Would you be able to mentally eliminate points from your final outline if the allotted interview time was shortened at the last second?   Yes _____ No _____

If you answered "no" to any of these questions—try practicing your PLC skills by asking a friend to interview you. (See "The Value of Practice" in this Part.)

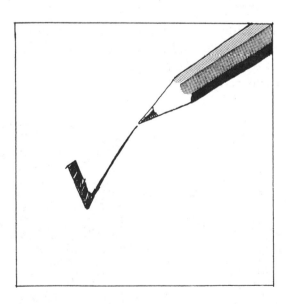

ANTICIPATING QUESTIONS

Now that you have set your goals for the interview, it's time to focus on the goals of the interviewer(s).

Sometimes, though very seldom, you will be supplied with a list of questions that the interviewer is planning to ask. Use such a list as general information only. Don't rely on it for the totality of your preparation. Certainly, go over all the questions on the list and be able to answer them fully, but prepare in the same methodical manner you would had no list been given to you. No matter what has been told to you before the program, an interviewer is liable to ask any question, from the most probing and incisive to the most ridiculously senseless and illogical.

You cannot, of course, anticipate the off-the-wall, stupid question. But you should never be surprised by any reasonable question asked you in a scheduled interview for which you've had time to prepare. Further, by the time you have reached the ''professional media interviewee'' level, you should not be surprised by any question asked of you—even in an abrupt, unscheduled interview as you leave your home, work, the courthouse, or a theatre.

When you master the techniques in this book, you'll have a mindset that will help you think from the media viewpoint. You will anticipate the logical questions to be asked about the day's developments, and even *when* the media will arrive to ask those questions.

The best training in reaching such a mindset is disciplining yourself to write down the most challenging and logical questions you're likely to be asked given all the facts and circumstances associated with the subject matter of the program and your participation.

ANTICIPATING QUESTIONS CHECKLIST

Honestly and completely respond to the following:

1. The question that would be potentially the most damaging to my company (or cause) is: _____

   _____

2. The question that would be the most challenging to me personally is: ____

   _____

3. The subject I'd most like to avoid is: _____

   _____

4. The reason I'd like to avoid that subject is: _____

   _____

5. The question that would require the most research on my part is: _____

   _____

6. Given the nature of my company (or cause), the general climate within the industry (or toward my viewpoint), and recent pertinent news stories, the most logical question an interviewer could ask me is: _____

   _____

7. The most intelligent question in relation to the environment and my organization's products or services (or my cause) is: _____

   _____

8. As background to set up the entire interview for the audience, the most likely question to be asked is: _____

   _____

9. The most difficult or delicate question I could be asked about my own personal opinion is: _____

   _____

10. A likely question about the most controversial aspect of my organization's activities (or my own personal responsibilities or manner of operating) is:

    _____

YOUR ANSWERS ➡

YOUR ANSWERS

In the spaces below, write your answers to the questions you have anticipated (except numbers 3 and 4). Your answers should be honest and positive. They should be as complete as possible without being too long.

1. _____
_____
_____
_____
_____
_____

2. _____
_____
_____
_____
_____
_____

5. _____
_____
_____
_____
_____
_____

6. _____
_____
_____
_____
_____
_____

7. _____
_____
_____
_____
_____
_____

8. _____
_____
_____
_____
_____
_____

9. _____
_____
_____
_____
_____
_____

10. _____
_____
_____
_____
_____
_____

THE VALUE OF PRACTICE

At this point in your preparation process you have gathered all the facts you can about the program and personnel involved, and determined your goals in the interview. You have come up with all the reasonable questions you think could be asked and have written out complete answers to those questions.

Sometimes the questions you anticipate are quite compatible with your goals. Most times, there is a degree of incompatibility. The last step in your preparation process is to practice with a friend who substitutes for the actual media interviewer. Your goal is to get your points across. The ''interviewer's'' goal is to pursue answers to the questions you expect to be asked.

The value of practicing for an upcoming interview cannot be overstated. Even media veterans need to practice. *There is a great difference between going over answers in your head and actually having to verbalize your responses.* And practice is the only way to determine if your goals are planted firmly enough to remember them while conversing about other matters.

A further important benefit of practice is training yourself to become more aware of the passage of time. You will do much better in a television interview if you're able to gauge accurately how much remains of the time you were allotted. Practice builds a level of confidence that will allow you to relax and show more of your personality to the viewers. Preparation is not complete without practice!

PRACTICE TIPS

1. Choose a person who is serious about helping you, one who will do her or his best in playing the interviewer's role.

2. If the subject matter of the interview is to be about business, it's ideal to have someone from your company act as the interviewer.

3. Supply the interviewer with your list of anticipated questions. Have the interviewer mix up the list and rephrase the questions in his or her own style.

4. Instruct the interviewer to hammer at getting those questions answered. The interviewer should, however, feel free to digress and ask whatever related questions come to mind.

5. Fully answer each of the interviewer's questions, but try to redirect the interview back to your agenda of prioritized points.

6. Set a firm time limit that closely approximates what you expect to be given on the program.

7. Practice with as many interviewers as possible.

8. If you can, videotape or audiotape each interview so that you can critique your answers. Pay particular attention to how you made your main points regardless of the questioning.

9. Never start over due to a mistake; go straight ahead as you would have to do on-the-air.

10. Work to shorten your answers. (In a broadcast interview that you know will be edited, a short comment that clearly makes a point is apt to be used. Such comments and answers have come to be known as ''sound bites.'')

FINAL CONSIDERATIONS

The following are points that are sometimes overlooked as the time draws near for your appearance. If they appear obvious, that speaks well for you. It is amazing how many people miss the obvious and put themselves at a disadvantage going into the interview.

- Be sure to supply complete biographical information about yourself, your accomplishments, your background and experience—positive points about you—to the interviewer or production staff. Normally, you're asked to supply this information. Even if you're not asked, supply it anyway, and make sure it's of high quality in content and form. Many times an interviewer has not prepared an introduction for you and will lift something from your material almost verbatim. Print interviewers also rely heavily on the material given to them.

- Occasionally, an interviewer will ask you how you would like to be introduced. Have an introduction in mind that is accurate and interesting.

- Do not be pompous about your title, position, or degrees. If you are a Ph.D., go by your first name after the introduction.

- If you have a difficult name, title, or position, make the pronunciation clear to the interviewer before going on-the-air. It is embarrassing to both the interviewer and you if the interview begins with a mistake. The inexperienced person never knows quite what to do at this time. None of the alternatives is very appealing.

• On the day of the interview, while waiting with other guests prior to the program, or when talking with a program staff member or assistant, *don't deliver your whole interview before it actually begins!* Don't talk too much about the content of the interview just prior to going on-the-air or beginning your conversation with a writer. If you do talk at length about the interview just before it begins, you are using energy best left for the actual interview. Worse, you may become confused as to what you have or haven't said during the interview. And if the interview involves other guests, they should hear your comments and opinions for the first time when you are broadcasting or taping, not before.

• Send a suggested list of questions to the interviewer or staff contact, perhaps at the same time you send your biographical material. These questions should cover the subject matter of the interview and lead to your main points. Often an interviewer will use some of your questions.

WHAT TO WEAR

We are all familiar with the saying, ''You only get one chance to make a good first impression.'' Combine the truth of that statement with the title and premise of William Thourlby's successful book, *You Are What You Wear: The Key to Business Success,* and you'll form a sound attitude about the importance of dressing properly for media interviews.

The first impression you make on television is a visual one. Viewers will start to form an opinion of you right away based solely on your appearance. The interviewer and the production staff will form immediate opinions of you also. And their opinions have a great deal to do with how you will be treated, how you'll do on-the-air, and whether you'll be asked back.

For television, you must consider the importance of what you wear, and your overall appearance, from two viewpoints: that of the viewers and that of the media staff. For radio and print, dress to make the right impression on the staff. It's more important than you may think. What you wear tells everyone involved who and what you are as an interview subject.

A good rule of thumb for all media is that, if you are being interviewed on behalf of your company, what you wear at work every day is appropriate. you should be comfortable in what you wear, generally on the conservative side, always clean, neat, and well-groomed. Of course, if an article or television interview is a personal profile of you at home, you'd dress differently than if the interview was strictly on business matters at your office.

Another good rule is that being too casual could cause you to be incorrectly perceived. Being too businesslike for a business interview is less likely to be to your disadvantage.

Use your own good judgment in making exceptions to the general rules. Perhaps you'll want to appear casual, perhaps your cause (or service, or product, or book) dictates a particular type of appearance. The point is, you *are* what you wear; so what you wear should correspond with how you want media people, viewers, and readers of articles with photos to perceive you.

WHAT-TO-WEAR GUIDELINES
FOR TELEVISION

- No stripes or checks (pinstripe suits are exceptions).

- No large, conspicuous, gaudy jewelry (both women and men).

- No bold patterns.

- No obvious focal point in your clothing that draws the eye to it.

- Generally no more than one subtle pattern (you may mix two subtle patterns of small areas, such as a tie with the shirt area that will be showing with your coat on).

- No clashing or loud colors, especially bright red.

- Try to avoid black and white together (off-white and grey are good).

- The perfect TV shirt is light blue. Any shirt worn with a coat should be lighter in color than the coat (unless you want to look like a member of the Mafia).

- Women, never wear a skirt or dress that makes it difficult to sit in a manner that denotes a businesslike demeanor.

- Men, never wear a vest on television.

- When seated, a man should unbutton his coat. If he is overweight, this will not look good—but keeping the coat buttoned looks worse. Don't let the coat open wide; show as little shirt as possible. One way to alleviate this entire problem is to wear a double-breasted jacket and leave it open. It will cover most of the shirt—and most of an ample stomach as well.

- If in doubt about what to wear, take two or three changes (all suitable to your image) to the studio and have the producer or director choose.

A WORD ABOUT MAKE-UP

Except for network and nationally syndicated programs, you will normally do your own make-up. Make-up should look natural and even. If you look made-up, you probably have on too much make-up.

Don't over-rely on make-up people. Take a good look at yourself before going on; if you don't like what you see, do something about it. If your cheeks are too rosy or your eyebrows too heavy or extended, tactfully ask the make-up person to remove some of the make-up—or go to the restroom and do it yourself.

If you perspire easily (or are bald), politely ask the make-up person to be standing by with some powder just before you go on and during commercial breaks.

You want to look like yourself at your healthy best, and this is what make-up should do for you. It is used to give your skin a smooth, even texture and color, free of oiliness and shine. Some men may need make-up to cover heavy beard shadow. Most television guests, men and women, need very little make-up. Some need none at all. Better too little than too much!

PART

VI

The Interview

If you thoroughly know your subject and if you have confidence because you have prepared and practiced for the most difficult of interviewers and questions, a media interview can actually be an enjoyable and satisfying experience. Sometimes it can be downright exhilarating. Even though you are dealing with a professional using that person's medium of communication, and most times their home turf, *you have some important and unquestionable advantages over the interviewer.* They should make you smile!

1. No matter how well the interviewer has done his or her homework, *you will always know infinitely more about your business and business position or cause!*

2. You can think much faster than the interviewer can talk.

3. It is virtually impossible for a straightforward, pleasant, and cooperative person who looks and/or sounds professional to make a negative impression on an audience.

4. You know exactly what you want to get across in the interview. You know the full facts, the good news, the positive aspects of your business or cause.

5. No reasonable question should come as a surprise. In fact, you should be able to think of many more questions specific to the subject than the interviewer's research could ever have developed.

6. If an unreasonable question is asked of you, audience members or readers will normally recognize it and not expect you to dignify the question with an unblinking response. They will expect a reaction and answer appropriate to the question.

THE INTERVIEW (Continued)

7. You have no obligation to keep an interview moving. That is the interviewer's responsibility. You don't have to keep talking once you've fully answered a question or made a point. "Dead air" on radio and TV broadcasts is not your concern and cannot make you look bad to the audience. (If appropriate, use a long pause to move on to another main point.)

8. You are under no obligation to tell something that is damaging to you or to your business or cause, or to reveal information helpful to your competitors.

9. You can make positive points to your advantage regardless of the pattern of questioning or the interviewer's lack of intelligence or preparedness.

10. One or two memorable comments by you can be of inestimable benefit to you and your company. On television and radio, the audience will hear those comments. (Unfortunately, in a print article the readers may or may not read them, depending upon the writer's decisions.)

11. On television and radio, if the interviewer interrupts often or doesn't allow you to answer fully, or is generally rude and obnoxious, the audience will recognize what's happening—and their sympathy will quickly go to you.

12. By virtue of being interviewed, you develop instant credibility and importance. In fact, you are perceived as being much more important than the interviewer. You are *needed* by the media. Think of yourself in this way.

PRODUCTION AND STAFF PERSONNEL

Do your best in a sincere way to be pleasant to all the personnel with whom you come in contact. Production and staff people can be of great assistance to you on the day of the media event. They have the answers to practically all the questions you might ask, and they will be helpful in their own rushed way if treated in a pleasant, professional, non-demanding manner.

Be prepared to deal with a wide variety of types of all ages and levels of experience. And keep in mind that these people have some input as to whether or not you will be used again.

SPEAKING OFF THE RECORD

```
❋ ❋ ❋ ❋ ❋ ❋ ❋ ❋ ❋ ❋ ❋ ❋ ❋ ❋ ❋
❋                              ❋
❋   An open foe may prove a curse;   ❋
❋     A pretended friend is worse.    ❋
❋                              ❋
❋        THE FARMER'S ALMANAC        ❋
❋                              ❋
❋ ❋ ❋ ❋ ❋ ❋ ❋ ❋ ❋ ❋ ❋ ❋ ❋ ❋ ❋
```

No matter what his or her level of competency, you can be sure that every media interviewer will be trying to get you to talk very candidly. No two media personalities are the same; but each has a well-practiced, sometimes quite subtle, technique for warmly gaining your cooperation or intimidating you by confrontation.

Certainly many media people with whom you will come in contact are wonderful human beings with a deep sense of honesty and fairness. Some are not! The important point is that, from a short meeting (and sometimes even from a long association), you cannot always tell the difference.

Some interviewers will act as though they truly are your friends. Keep in mind that you are not being interviewed to build friendships. Your goal in every interview is to advance the image and positive aspects of your organization, idea, or cause, and to heighten your own stature as an important shaper of public thought.

Never be so taken in by a member of the media (whether an on-air personality, producer, staff member, writer, or administrator) that you will reveal any bit of information you would not proudly announce on the Network Evening News. Make it a hard and fast rule that absolutely nothing you say is off the record. Anything you say may be used later in some way, so don't be drawn in by people who say or imply that they will honor your definition of what's on and what's off the record. Answer reasonable questions fully and honestly, but keep to yourself what should be kept private.

> Never speak off the record.

THE OBVIOUS—PART 1

There is a lot you need to be aware of in connection with interviews. Some points are obvious—such as that you shouldn't have a drink just before the interview. List any other obvious points that occur to you:

_____

_____

_____

_____

_____

_____

_____

_____

_____

_____

_____

_____

_____

_____

_____

_____

_____

_____

_____

_____

_____

_____

_____

THE OBVIOUS—PART 2

Listed below are rock-bottom requirements. If you listed most of them, you're doing well—but there's more to come!

- No drinking of alcoholic beverages prior to the interview.

- No smoking while on television.

- Curtail any nervous mannerisms, if possible.

- No meaningless expressions such as ''and so on and so forth'' or ''and things like that.''

- No wisecracking or joking during the interview unless you are an accomplished performer.

- If sitting, sit up straight, conveying a sense of interest and urgency.

- If standing, your posture should reflect that same interest and sense of urgency.

- Be sincere and enthusiastic.

- Look at the interviewer when talking with him or her—not a lock stare, merely normal attentiveness.

- On television, if there is a studio audience, look at them when appropriate.

- Don't play to TV cameras unless you are very experienced or are answering a telephone call and have been told which camera is for that purpose.

- Arrive early or be free when media people arrive at your location. Don't keep media people waiting.

THE SUBSTANCE

The media are still evolving and developing. Formats, customs, styles, and general paradigms are forming and reforming within the industry. Constant change (sometimes even back to earlier days) is a major aspect of the media.

No one person or book is a repository of all the collected wisdom regarding media interviews. No one knows all the techniques and little tricks for dealing smoothly and effectively with any situation that might arise to challenge an interviewee. However, experienced broadcasters, journalists, image makers, critical observers, and successful media guests have compiled an abundance of solid information. It can be put together to form a valid composite picture of the effective media interviewee.

The following is a list of interview guidelines—what you should and should not do to be effective. When combined with thorough preparation and practice, following the guidelines will greatly enhance your overall performance and the impact you make both on the audience and on members of the media.

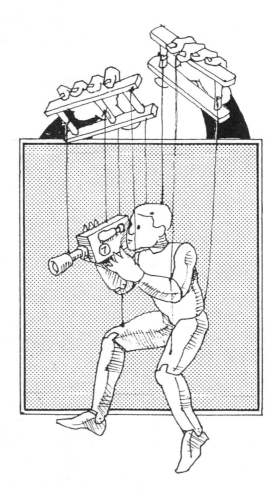

INTERVIEW GUIDELINES

- Never lie!

- Be yourself. Don't try to develop a different persona for media interviews. Don't attempt to become what you think you should be as a media guest. Develop yourself. Rely on the strong points of your own character, personality and experiences for raw materials.

- Stress the positive aspects of your company, your cause, your ideas. Relate good news and helpful information as much as possible.

- Settle on what you think is a proper and comfortable way to address the interviewer. Opinions of experts vary on this matter. Some say never use the interviewer's first name. Do what is most sincere and spontaneous for you, but don't get too chummy. Doing so will weaken your position with the audience. This advice is for news and business-oriented subject matter. Certainly, friendly exchanges are appropriate for many topics on talk shows and for light, informational articles.

- Keep your message simple. Comments should be brief, to the point, and easily understood by the general public and the media people with whom you are dealing. If you do this, your words are more likely to be remembered and you'll have more time to make more points. Long, rambling answers and comments should be avoided.

- Don't use jargon peculiar to your trade, profession, or group. If you must use terms not generally known to everyone, briefly define or explain them.

- It's always better to say something important more than once than to say several unimportant things.

- Don't try to make too many complex points, especially in a television interview.

- You are not in an interview to defend yourself. Don't allow yourself to be put in such a position. Worse yet, don't assume it!

- Don't be afraid of not answering a question, but explain why you can't. Viewers, listeners and readers don't expect anyone to know everything. If otherwise credible, you will many times gain added credibility by saying ''I don't feel qualified to answer that,'' or ''I'd like to leave that up to the experts,'' or ''I don't have the complete data at this time.'' As long as it's obvious that you're not trying to be evasive, you become more believable in general by admitting there are things you don't know.

INTERVIEW GUIDELINES (Continued)

- Know your ground and don't be sidetracked. Don't allow the interviewer to take up valuable time on matters that are unimportant or unrelated to your goals.

- In general, the tougher the question, the shorter should be your answer and the calmer your demeanor.

- Never lose your temper. Don't shout or yell. Always remain calm and courteous. The more inflammatory the interviewer or fellow panel member, the cooler you should be. Remain firm in your comments and always in control.

- Don't volunteer information or opinions that may damage you.

- Refute incorrect statements. Immediately correct any statement that is inaccurate, especially if the statement weakens your position. This includes statements made by anyone—the interviewer, other guests, audience members, callers—even you. If you do make a meaningful error, admit it, apologize, quickly explain, and then go on.

- Don't let the interviewer misinterpret your statements. Politely interrupt and set the interviewer straight as to your meaning.

- Don't legitimize loaded words by repeating them. In your response either point out the loaded words or change them so as to disarm them.

- Keep in mind that you don't have to use the words used by the interviewer. Paraphrase the interviewer's questions or comments in such a way that it will better suit your purpose.

- Don't let the interviewer interrupt often. If you raise your voice slightly, then continue, most radio and television personalities will back off. The exception is the host who is known for harrassing guests. If you've done your homework, you'll know about this fact long before your appearance on the program.

- You may ask questions of the interviewer for various reasons—for clarification, to direct her question back to her (''What would you have done?''), or to buy time to think as you formulate an idea. Don't hesitate to use this device. It's effective, a change of pace, and most interviewers like it since it draws attention to them.

- Once you have fully answered a question or made a point, stop talking. Don't be pushed into adding something that is unnecessary or that you don't want to add just because the interviewer remains silent. Inexperienced media guests are sometimes fooled by this technique. It's an attempt to get you to reveal information beyond what you intend.

- Don't be sucked in by hypothetical or leading questions. Turn them aside with ''I wouldn't want to speculate on that,'' or ''I find that discussing hypothetical situations takes time and energy away from more important real-life situations,'' or ''That's really a leading question, and I find that a leading question often leads to a misleading answer.''

- Provide evidence to support your points and claims. For example, don't say ''We're concerned for the safety of your children,'' or ''We are very ecologically conscious,'' unless you can describe actions by you or your company that bear out such statements.

- Develop or locate anecdotes, analogies, quotes, and metaphors that illustrate and enliven the points you want to make. People love stories. Think up a slogan or easily remembered catch phrase that plants an idea in the minds of audience members or readers.

- Have a ready supply of visuals (photos, videotape, film clips, charts, illustrations) for television producers, audio tapes for radio producers, and high quality photos and other materials for print journalists and writers. Naturally, only have available materials that will strongly aid you in reaching your interview goals. You do not want to use anything that merely takes up time or space. The media people may or may not use your material, but it is best to have it available. TV, radio, and print decision makers are always looking to add variety in a program or article.

- Let the viewers or listeners know if you're surprised on a program by material that is not yours and that you didn't expect and had no opportunity to peruse before the program.

- Normally you should have no notes or papers with you during a television interview unless some very specific and complex information is to be discussed. Don't read prepared answers or statements. Exceptions might be some press conferences where you are making specific public statements on behalf of an organization or directly quoting someone.

INTERVIEW GUIDELINES (Continued)

- During any type of media interview, don't allow distractions to throw you. Crew conversations, background motion, and other extraneous noises are easy to disregard if you expect and anticipate them.

- When dealing with other guests or panel members during an interview, treat them with dignity and courtesy no matter how they behave. Be assertive, but not overbearing, in getting your share of the time allotted. Try not to interrupt or contribute to otherwise disruptive behavior. Politely but firmly get the time you need.

- It's good to show genuine emotion, but don't allow the emotion to take over. Laugh, cry, show surprise, disappointment, even indignation, if doing so helps you accomplish your goals in the interview or shows a positive facet of your character. Just don't let an emotion cause a flood of words that will detract from your message or image.

- During an interview, don't be afraid to repeat a key point in slightly different words.

- Sometimes possessing a great deal of knowledge on a subject makes people forget to simplify. Always strive to simplify all your comments and answers.

- Try to have the last word in a television or radio interview. Don't allow the interviewer to end on a note negative to you and your interests.

- Sit still and in place at the end of a television interview until you are certain that you are off-the-air and that your microphone is off. Make no additional comments! The same audio rule applies to radio interviews.

- Being in control is important, but trying to be in control may cause you to tighten up. Control does not result from trying. A natural form of control results from the quiet confidence and calmness that you develop in knowing that you have thoroughly prepared and practiced.

- Never lie! (This is worth repeating)

TIME MANAGEMENT

You might imagine that time will pass slowly during a media interview. You will find that quite the contrary is true. No matter what the length, time will pass very quickly. You must develop a sense of elapsed time and learn to manage it to your advantage.

In a print interview, time may seem of less concern since there is no audience of viewers or listeners and you don't have the pressures of broadcast time constraints. Don't be fooled; print interviews have their time limitations too. You had better know how much time the person interviewing you has allotted for the two of you to talk.

Certainly, the time may be extended, but don't count on it. Proceed as you would with a radio or TV interview and budget your time so that it will not run out before you've attained your goals. Obviously, you can keep track of the time by checking your watch or a clock.

During a radio interview surprises can occur. If the program is thirty minutes or an hour in length, don't expect to get all that time. Always ask how much time you should subtract for commercials and other time-consuming items such as weather reports and public service announcements. You should also ask whether the host has a routine to close the show and how long the routine is.

Try to find out just how many minutes you actually have. Also, without being offensive or trying to run the program, try to get an idea at least of how the host normally wraps up the show. Be conscious of how much time you've used and how much still remains. Work toward your prioritized goals accordingly.

Television programs, television and radio news interviews, and abrupt television and radio confrontations are the real challenges. During scheduled television programs, time cues are normally given only to the host. Seldom does a guest receive any time cues. Clocks are usually nowhere to be seen and looking at your watch gives a negative impression.

During a short news interview, whether live or taped, the news reporter may cut a guest off in mid-sentence if a previous comment has met the reporter's needs. Similarly, the abrupt confrontational interview may end at any point at the discretion of the reporter holding the microphone.

Some broadcast interviewers, especially on longer scheduled programs, will give you an indication that time is winding down. Most won't. The ones who do will sometimes let you summarize by asking "Is there anything we haven't covered?" or "In closing, anything you'd like to add?" or "What are the main points you'd like our viewers/listeners to take from this interview?"

TIME MANAGEMENT (Continued)

A few hosts will merely say something like ''We have thirty seconds left.'' This is your cue to quickly recap or make an important point you have not already made.

On television and radio news interviews where the reporter has given you no indication of how much time you will have, or when you are confronted abruptly by a TV or radio reporter, make your most important point at the first opportunity.

On television talk shows, public service programs, and scheduled news programs of some length, don't let more than what you sense is one-third of your time pass without making one of your top points. Don't sit back too long expecting the interviewer to present you with exactly the questions or opportunities you want. If the opportunities do not present themselves early in the interview, make your own opportunities within the flow of the conversation before your time expires.

Practicing interviews of varying lengths with different people is the key to developing a sense of elapsed time.

CONVERSATIONAL MANEUVERING

To the uninitiated, the most difficult and challenging part of the entire media experience appears to be those crucial minutes (or hours) when you will be talking with the media person in the actual interview. You picture yourself dry-mouthed and groping for words that make sense, trying to concentrate while resisting the urge to get up and flee the scene.

In this book, you will notice that more space is devoted to ''Before the Interview'' than to any other area. This is truly the most difficult and challenging part of the entire media experience. You are much more likely to make errors, especially errors of omission, in the preparation phase. And there is a tendency to be lazy and unfocused in practice.

If, however, you have thoroughly prepared and practiced, you will be quite comfortable during the interview and, more important, *you will be effective.*

Each of you reading this book possesses a style of speaking and acting and reacting unique to you. Given the same interviewer and subject, interviews of any two of you would not be the same. This very fact is what keeps the media in business and provides such great diversity in programming and in print articles.

People want to see, hear and read about a wide variety of media guests being comfortably themselves. No one wants to see and hear automatons on TV and radio, or read the same comments in print over and over again. The public wants to identify with, and be entertained and informed by, genuine people spontaneously and honestly responding to the live stimuli of one another.

You will be most effective in an interview when you have molded your own style of speaking, acting and reacting to fit the conditions and restrictions of each medium. It helps to watch experienced politicians, entertainers and media regulars whom you admire for their answers and quickness of thought. But it should never be your goal to actually be like anyone else or to answer as they would.

Your goal should be to get yourself into an interview-useful pattern of thinking. Then allow your natural conversational style to reflect that thinking. The core of the thinking pattern is this:

- The most important goal is to make your main points.

- The second goal is to fully answer questions in a way that makes a positive impression.

- Both of these goals can be achieved by being prepared and attentive, and by bridging thoughts and redirecting the conversation.

THOUGHT STIMULATORS

The best media trainers seldom supply actual answers and comments for people to use in interviews. Incorrect answers and inappropriate comments are pointed out during practice, but words are not put into people's mouths. When left to their own styles and response times, even inexperienced people *(provided they are thoroughly prepared)* do better in interviews using their own words and natural thought processes.

Keeping in mind what was just said, the following answers, comments and exchanges are included only to stimulate your thinking. They may help you in phrasing your answers or comments and in redirecting the conversation.

- When possible, especially if the subject matter is of concern to the general public, frame your comments and answers in the context of ''the public interest''—''increased employment''— ''quality of life''— ''community benefits''—''help for the greatest numbers''—and similar positive and evocative terms. Audiences *feel* more than they *think*. Facts may escape them at times, but feelings seldom do.

- Don't say ''We're aware of those complaints and are checking into them.'' Say rather ''We're sensitive to those concerns.'' Then tell how your company's sensitivity is reflected in action.

- A possible way to begin an answer: ''Before I can answer that question fully, a little background is necessary.'' While giving the necessary background, you also make one of your main points. Or you could begin by saying ''To put my answer to that question in context, a few facts first.'' There are numerous similar ways to both answer a question and make a main point or two.

- If you are presented with a less-than-great question, don't put the interviewer down! You might respond with: ''That's a good question, and I'll answer it; but our research has shown that the public is not really concerned with that aspect of the problem.'' Or you could say: ''That's a good question, but do you know the one that most of our customers ask?''

- The owner of a small radio station asked the manager of a local drugstore: ''Where are you located and what services do you provide?'' (Yes, people do ask such questions. What an open-ended opportunity for free advertising!) The manager began his answer by giving the street address of the store, then dryly listed ''prescriptions, stationery, magazines,'' and so on.

His answer should have been: ''You can't miss us, we're right next to the movie theater (the only one in town) with that big parking area in front of our store.'' Naturally, he should list his major services, but he should use some of the time given him to stress the courtesy and helpfulness of his employees. Always add something positive about your cause, service or product if given the opportunity.

- Two businessmen were being interviewed on a morning network news program. One man headed the nation's largest soup company. The interviewer asked him about his view of the country's economic woes. Before he became specific about the direction of the economy as a whole, the soup man said: ''I know there's supposed to be a recession out there; but, can you believe, we sold more mushroom soup this year than in any year in the sixty-year history of being this country's sales leader!''

- Again on a national television broadcast, a prominent clergyman, a leader in his denomination, was asked about ''the biggest crisis facing the church today.'' He quickly responded: ''I see no crisis, I see opportunities.'' He then went on to tell of the growing number of people coming into the church and of the challenge of bringing the church's teachings to many diverse nationalities.

- A member of a political party was asked: ''What do you have to do to get to the White House?'' He answered: ''It's very hard to reinvent a political party. We get to the White House by turning from the past to a more moderate philosophy.'' He went on to explain what he meant. Do you think that this guest was prepared? Did he anticipate the question or did that first clever sentence just pop into his mind?

THOUGHT STIMULATORS (Continued)

- In a major city, annual free training in CPR (cardiopulmonary resuscitation) is offered to the public. The program has been very successful, drawing a few thousand people each year over a two-day period. Each of the more than one hundred CPR experts works one-on-one with anyone who wants to learn the lifesaving techniques.

  A TV reporter, surveying the extensive preparations in the large gymnasium, asked the person in charge, "I know that things can become like a madhouse around here with so many people coming and going, and all the training going on. Any advice?"

  The interviewee, sensing the negative tone of the word "madhouse" and how it could impact people who were considering making the effort to attend, looked directly into the camera and said confidently and enthusiastically, "Do come!" She then went on to offer good advice about leaving toddlers at home, and so on.

  The point here is that the guest immediately erased a negative feeling with a dynamic two-word positive statement. She did not dwell on the troublesome aspects of attending, as the reporter's phrasing might have led her to do.

Are you beginning to absorb and understand what it means to think positively and creatively, to develop opportunities to reach your goals, and to use the interview conversation for your own purposes? Preparation, practice, and the correct thinking pattern will result in making your style effective.

VII

After the Interview

The first thing you should do after any interview is to thank the people involved. Most of the time, it's very easy to be motivated to do this. Many of the people will have been helpful and pleasant, and you'll want to thank them.

There will, however, be times that you will not feel like thanking anyone. You may be in a bad mood about your own performance, or disappointed in the interviewer or staff or crew. Nevertheless, thank everyone who is conveniently near and available. Even seek out those who have been particularly helpful—for example, the TV director who is in the booth, or the person in the office who helped you get situated when you first arrived.

There is more than one way to say thank you. To those people who have been especially cordial and helpful, you'll be more enthusiastic and sincere. There is, however, a professional manner of thanking even those people you haven't dealt with or those who have made your appearance less successful or pleasant than you would have liked. Never allow yourself to drop below this level of professionalism. You will be remembered for it, sometimes by the least likely person who could help you later.

After a print interview, ask the writer if you may read the article before it is published. Politely make it clear that you are only checking for accuracy of what you said or didn't say that you might like to add. Never say or imply that you are concerned with a writer's style or interpretation or analysis of what you said. Usually you won't get the chance to read the article, but it's worth asking. When you do get the chance, you can sometimes tactfully affect needed changes.

AFTER THE INTERVIEW (Continued)

If a crew has videotaped or filmed at your office, plant or home, and will be editing the material for a feature to be shown at a later date, ask to see the final edited piece before it's shown. Ask right after the shooting has taken place. You may be allowed some input. Though you probably won't, it's still worth asking.

No interview is perfect. After an interview, especially a relatively short one, it's normal to feel a bit disappointed. The tendency is to second-guess yourself. Don't waste time doing this. Conversely, don't let yourself get too elated after a great interview that went all your way. Keep on an even keel.

Build up a supply of videotapes, audiotapes, articles and pictures that demonstrate your best work, your style, your expertise in a certain area. When you feel you've done particularly well on a broadcast, ask the producer for a tape of the program. Offer to pay for it—or supply the correct format tape prior to the broadcast if it is an important one.

Contact the print writer who originally interviewed you, or the circulation department of the publication, for copies of articles involving you. Flattering photos or photos with important people who could enhance your popularity or prestige should be obtained also.

These media materials are tools for obtaining more exposure. It is wise to keep updating them, even to the point of having your best recent television and radio appearances edited into *brief* composite video and audio tapes.

Viewing or listening to tapes of your appearances, or rereading articles in which your words are featured, is a much different activity than second-guessing. In privacy, you should occasionally take time to analyze past participation in media events, but don't dwell on trivial points. Look for indications of not being properly prepared, not dressing appropriately, not listening attentively, missing opportunities to make a main point, your apparent comfort level, and other major points. Learn from the past, but don't live in it.

Keep a journal and, after each media appearance, write down all the pertinent information about it. Be punctilious about recording the names and positions of major players in the event, especially those who impressed you or on whom you sense you made a good impression. Be sure to include any other guests or panel members in your journal. Any or all of these people could help you in the future. There is a great deal of movement within the industry. Keep track of people who move up or out to another media outlet.

P A R T

VIII

Initiating Media Contact

You don't have to wait for the media to come to you. It's not difficult to call or write to a television or radio station or the offices of a newspaper, magazine or trade journal. Making contact is fairly simple and easy. Finding the right person to consider your idea, product, service or cause will normally be less simple and less easy. Actually being on-the-air or getting print coverage will require considerable time and effort. But the return can be enormous.

The keys to being successful in developing your own participation in media events are good ideas and persistence. Even though the media are always looking for new ideas and people for programs and articles, your suggestions must stand out above the many that are submitted to producers, writers, news directors and hosts. You must anticipate that you will frequently be turned down. But if your idea is turned down by one person or one medium, another person or medium might love it and be in need at the time you make contact.

You must package your idea (and yourself) in an attractive manner, either by the type of letter you first write and the additional material you send with it, or by a confident, well-phrased "sell job" when you first talk on the telephone with the right person.

Television, radio, and print people don't have much time to spend talking with someone they don't know, or reading unsolicited material. So you and your material had better be especially good at getting attention. One way of getting attention is to have someone else make the first contact for you, recommending you and telling what's exciting about you or your idea.

INITIATING MEDIA CONTACT (Continued)

Naturally, if you have already made broadcast appearances or been featured in publications, you will have a distinct advantage. You'll also have material to show your competency or popularity level.

When dealing with a radio or television station, try to make contact with the producer of the actual program on which you want to participate. If your idea is news oriented, contact the news director. With newspapers and magazines, try to contact an actual writer, one who covers the subject area in which your idea would be included. With trade journals, contact the editor. In any of these cases, if you cannot get to the person you want, speak courteously with (or write to) a subordinate, outlining your proposal. If you get that person's interest and cooperation, he or she can be of great assistance to you.

If the persons who will make the decisions about your possible participation ask for any additional material, respond promptly. Offer to meet with them, more than once if necessary. Be cooperative and professional in every way. Make certain that every idea you present is well thought out and that all your material exudes class and organization.

Keep in mind the turnover rate mentioned earlier. If you have not met with success, wait a short time, then resubmit your idea to the same media outlet.

You will have your best chance of success when you match your message to the appropriate medium. If what you're trying to get before the public is very visual in content, direct all your efforts to getting television exposure. If your idea or cause involves considerable history and details that would lend themselves to a rather lengthy conversation and then audience questions, contact radio stations to be on a one-hour talk show with call-ins.

You will immediately know if print, radio or TV is best. If all media are suitable, pursue them all with vigor and persistence.

REVIEW

By now it should be clear that dealing effectively with the media is within the capabilities of nearly everyone. No special personal quality or unique ability is necessary.

What is necessary is a particular mindset and a dedication to thorough preparation and practice. There is nothing complicated or difficult in the process. And there is absolutely no reason to be awed by the media or the people who work in the media.

As a final recap, critically evaluate yourself by answering the following questions. Check ''yes'' or ''no'' as appropriate.

Yes	No

_____ _____ **1.** Do I really believe that the media have enormous influence over people?

_____ _____ **2.** Am I convinced that participation in a media event could have a great impact on my career, business or cause?

_____ _____ **3.** Do I now consider myself knowledgeable about the media in general, its workings and its personnel?

_____ _____ **4.** Do I believe that most businesses can't disregard the media and still be successful?

_____ _____ **5.** Would I be willing to thoroughly research a program, publication or personality I might be involved with in a media event?

_____ _____ **6.** Would I be willing to give up some control and feel comfortable about adapting myself to the requirements of a particular medium?

_____ _____ **7.** Do I generally feel comfortable talking with others about myself, my work, my ideals, and other subjects about which I feel strongly?

_____ _____ **8.** Am I willing to study and put in the time to assimilate all the necessary information to make myself well-informed on an issue, product, service or cause?

REVIEW (Continued)

_____ _____ 9. Could I clearly write out what I'd like to get across to people if given the opportunity?

_____ _____ 10. Could I come up with questions that most people would want to ask about my area of expertise or interest?

_____ _____ 11. Am I willing to dedicate myself to practice until I feel comfortable in dealing with any question?

_____ _____ 12. Do I have a reasonably good short-term memory?

_____ _____ 13. Can I keep my composure when pressured?

_____ _____ 14. Would my friends and business associates describe me as showing good taste in how I dress?

_____ _____ 15. Am I a good listener?

_____ _____ 16. Do I enjoy new challenges?

_____ _____ 17. Can I visualize long-term benefits from present efforts?

Would a person who answered "yes" to all seventeen questions be an unusual individual? Certainly not. In fact, a person who answered "yes" to all the questions except the first four would pretty well typify an average, hard-working, mature-thinking person who is trying to get ahead at work and trying to develop positive and beneficial personality traits.

Anyone who would answer "no" to any of the first four questions is merely uninformed and needs to do more reading from the right sources.

Admittedly, no book can teach you everything there is to know about any subject that involves complex human interaction. However, you can learn a great deal, enough to develop yourself into a very effective media participant. The author and numerous other prominent media trainers are available for advanced help and practice for you and other people in your company, or for those who share your drive to get an idea across to the public.

But, make no mistake about it, if you master the techniques described in this book and dedicate yourself to thorough preparation and practice, _you will be very effective in all your dealings with any sector of the media at any level._

Don't waste the numerous media opportunities that will be available to you. Be prepared. Take advantage of the enormous influential power of the media.

SUGGESTED READING LIST

Ailes, Roger, *You Are The Message.* Dow Jones-Irwin, Homewood, Illinois 1988

Bagdikian, Ben, *The Media Monopoly.* Beacon Press, Boston 1987.

Decker, Bert, *The Art Of Communicating.* Crisp Publications, Los Altos, CA 1988

LaHaye, Tim, *The Hidden Censors.* Power Books, Fleming H. Revell Company, Old Tappan, NJ 1984

Lichter, Rothman, Lichter, *The Media Elite.* Adler & Adler, Bethesda, MD 1986

Mallory Charles, *Publicity Power.* Crisp Publications, Los Altos, CA 1989

Thourlby, William, *You Are What You Wear.* Forbes/Wittenburg & Brown, New York 1990.

NOTES

NOTES

NOTES

NOTES

NOW AVAILABLE FROM
CRISP PUBLICATIONS

Books • Videos • CD Roms • Computer-Based Training Products

If you enjoyed this book, we have great news for you. There are over 200 books available in the *50-Minute*™ Series. To request a free full-line catalog, contact your local distributor or Crisp Publications, Inc., 1200 Hamilton Court, Menlo Park, CA 94025. Our toll-free number is 800-442-7477.

Subject Areas Include:

Management
Human Resources
Communication Skills
Personal Development
Marketing/Sales
Organizational Development
Customer Service/Quality
Computer Skills
Small Business and Entrepreneurship
Adult Literacy and Learning
Life Planning and Retirement

CRISP WORLDWIDE DISTRIBUTION

English language books are distributed worldwide. Major international distributors include:

ASIA/PACIFIC

Australia/New Zealand: In Learning, PO Box 1051 Springwood QLD, Brisbane, Australia 4127
Telephone: 7-3841-1061, Facsimile: 7-3841-1580   ATTN: Messrs. Gordon

Singapore: Graham Brash (Pvt) Ltd. 32, Gul Drive, Singapore 2262
Telephone: 65-861-1336, Facsimile: 65-861-4815   ATTN: Mr. Campbell

CANADA

Reid Publishing, Ltd., Box 69559-109 Thomas Street, Oakville, Ontario Canada L6J 7R4.
Telephone: (905) 842-4428, Facsimile: (905) 842-9327   ATTN: Mr. Reid

Trade Book Stores: Raincoast Books, 8680 Cambie Street, Vancouver, British Columbia, Canada V6P 6M9.
Telephone: (604) 323–7100, Facsimile: 604-323-2600   ATTN: Ms. Laidley

EUROPEAN UNION

England: Flex Training, Ltd. 9-15 Hitchin Street, Baldock, Hertfordshire, SG7 6A, England
Telephone: 1-462-896000, Facsimile: 1-462-892417   ATTN: Mr. Willetts

INDIA

Multi-Media HRD, Pvt., Ltd., National House, Tulloch Road, Appolo Bunder, Bombay, India 400-039
Telephone: 91-22-204-2281, Facsimile: 91-22-283-6478   ATTN: Messrs. Aggarwal

MIDDLE EAST

United Arab Emirates: Al-Mutanabbi Bookshop, PO Box 71946, Abu Dhabi
Telephone: 971-2-321-519, Facsimile: 971-2-317-706   ATTN: Mr. Salabbai

SOUTH AMERICA

Mexico: Grupo Editorial Iberoamerica, Serapio Rendon #125, Col. San Rafael, 06470 Mexico, D.F.
Telephone: 525-705-0585, Facsimile: 525-535-2009   ATTN: Señor Grepe

SOUTH AFRICA

Alternative Books, Unit A3 Sanlam Micro Industrial Park, Hammer Avenue STRYDOM Park, Randburg, 2194 South Africa
Telephone: 2711 792 7730, Facsimile: 2711 792 7787   ATTN: Mr. de Haas